Elephant's Graveyard

by George Brant

A SAMUEL FRENCH ACTING EDITION

SAMUEL FRENCH

FOUNDED 1830

NEW YORK HOLLYWOOD LONDON TORONTO

SAMUELFRENCH.COM

ISBN 978-0-573-69815-6   Printed in U.S.A.   #29608

MUSIC USE NOTE

Licensees are solely responsible for obtaining formal written permission from copyright owners to use copyrighted music in the performance of this play and are strongly cautioned to do so. If no such permission is obtained by the licensee, then the licensee must use only original music that the licensee owns and controls. Licensees are solely responsible and liable for all music clearances and shall indemnify the copyright owners of the play and their licensing agent, Samuel French, Inc., against any costs, expenses, losses and liabilities arising from the use of music by licensees.

IMPORTANT BILLING AND CREDIT REQUIREMENTS

All producers of *ELEPHANT'S GRAVEYARD must* give credit to the Author of the Play in all programs distributed in connection with performances of the Play, and in all instances in which the title of the Play appears for the purposes of advertising, publicizing or otherwise exploiting the Play and/or a production. The name of the Author *must* appear on a separate line on which no other name appears, immediately following the title and *must* appear in size of type not less than fifty percent of the size of the title type.

In addition the following credit *must* be given in all programs and publicity information distributed in association with this piece:

Originally produced by Trustus Theatre, Columbia, South Carolina.
Jim Thigpen, Artistic Director.

ELEPHANT'S GRAVEYARD was first produced by the University of Texas at Austin in the Oscar Brockett Theatre in Austin, Texas on November 16, 2007. The performance was directed by Laura Kepley, with sets by Szu-Feng Chen, costumes by Jan McCauley, lighting by Jennifer Madison, dramaturgy by Erica Nagel. The production stage manager was Lori Grubbs. The cast was as follows:

PREACHER . . . . Neil Ames
GUITARIST . . . . James Betz
MUDDY TOWNSPERSON . . . . Lizzi Biggers
HUNGRY TOWNSPERSON . . . . Matrex Kilgore
STEAM SHOVEL OPERATOR . . . . Daniel Salmones
YOUNG TOWNSPERSON . . . . Shannon Schaefer
MARSHAL . . . . Tom Truss
RINGMASTER . . . . George Brant
BALLET GIRL . . . . Anna Fugate
TRAINER. . . . . Tim Longo
CLOWN . . . . Ben Schave
STRONGMAN . . . . Hunter Smith
DRUMMER . . . . Mark Smoot
TOUR MANAGER . . . . Shaun Tubbs
ENGINEER . . . . Keenan Zarling

ELEPHANT'S GRAVEYARD had its non-equity premiere at the Trustus Theatre in Columbia, South Carolina on May 1, 2009. The performance was directed by Robert Richmond, sound by Baxter Engle, with sets by Samantha Hayford, costumes by Valerie Pruett, lighting by Joe Laney. The production stage manager was Taylor Harrison. The cast was as follows:

RINGMASTER . . . . Michael Downey
TRAINER. . . . . Steven Kopp
BALLET GIRL . . . . Vicky Saye Henderson
TOUR MANAGER . . . . Gary Pozsik
STRONGMAN . . . . Will Moreau
CLOWN . . . . Alec Grooms
HUNGRY TOWNSPERSON . . . . Jabar K. Hankins
MARSHAL . . . . Scott Stepp
MUDDY TOWNSPERSON . . . . Robin Gottlieb
PREACHER . . . . Alex Smith
STEAM SHOVEL OPERATOR . . . . Bobby Bloom
YOUNG TOWNSPERSON . . . . Mary Tilden
GUITARIST . . . . Leisl Downey
ENGINEER . . . . Jonathan Jackson

ELEPHANT'S GRAVEYARD was the winner of the 2008 Keene Prize for Literature and 2008 David Mark Cohen National Playwriting Award

CHARACTERS

The Circus

    RINGMASTER – obsessed with the bottom line

    TRAINER – loves his work

    BALLET GIRL – a showgirl in control

    TOUR MANAGER – bit of a bully

    STRONGMAN – a proud muscleman from Europe's far-off shores

    CLOWN – a comedian with an inferiority complex

    DRUMMER – keeps the beat

The Town

    HUNGRY TOWNSPERSON – African-American, a steel-trap memory

    MARSHAL – keeps the peace

    MUDDY TOWNSPERSON – a haunted widow

    PREACHER – doggedly hopeful

    STEAM SHOVEL OPERATOR – looking for escape

    YOUNG TOWNSPERSON – excitable dreamer

    GUITARIST/HARMONICA PLAYER – sets the rhythm

The Railroad

    ENGINEER – confident Time is on his side

AUTHOR'S NOTES

Sound

All music and sound effects should be provided live by the Drummer and Guitarist (drum rolls, gunshots, train whistles, etc.). The Drummer is primarily an instrument of the circus; the Guitarist is primarily an instrument of the town.

Set

The set may be an empty stage or an abstract collision of the worlds of the circus, town and railroad. This collision need not be pretty.

Performance

The telling of this story must be active, a sort of present past, allowing for a full range of emotion; the end must not be played at the beginning.

Staging

If an action is described by the storytellers, it should not be shown. The staging of the play should complement the dialogue, not make it redundant.

Casting

Roles may be played by any race or gender except when specified.

Music

Companies are invited to create a melody for "*You Got to Lift It*" that suits their production. "*Standing on the Promises*" is a hymn in the Public Domain.

Special Thanks

Marla Akin, ATHE, Balagan Theatre, Chris Benson, Stephen Berenson, the Brants, Mark Charney, Sheila Daniels, Ron Daniels, Steven Dietz, Michael Evenden, Jake Groshong, Jason Harber, Gregg Henry, Daniel Alexander Jones, E.L. Keene, the Kennedy Center, Caitlin McLeod, James Magnuson, Denise Martel, Emily Morse, Erica Nagel, Charles Otte, Daniel Patterson, Charles Edwin Price, Robert Richmond, Judith Royer, Kate Snodgrass, Jim and Kay Thigpen, Adrienne Thompson, Trinity Repertory Company, Trustus Theatre, Jon Tuttle, Naomi Wallace, Craig Watson, David White, Dawn Youngs, Suzan Zeder, all the casts, crews, and designers who have worked on the play and my first and best reader, Laura Kepley.

Development

Elephant's Graveyard was developed with the generous assistance of the James A. Michener Center for Writers, The University of Texas at Austin, and WordBRIDGE Playwright's Lab.

"Friday I tasted life. It was a vast morsel. A Circus passed the house – still I feel the red in my mind though the drums are out."

– Emily Dickinson

For Mary

(The **DRUMMER** *and* **GUITARIST** *enter, taking their places. The* **GUITARIST** *sings a song in the Piedmont blues style,* **You Got To Lift It.***)*

GUITARIST.

You got trouble on your mind
You gotta lift it
'Fore it drives you blind
You gotta lift it
'Fore it leaks into your brain
Fixin' to drive you insane
Got to lift it
Lift it
Lift it off your mind

Got a monkey on your back
You gotta lift it
I'm'a tellin' you now, Jack
You gotta lift it
Lift it off or before it's through
Only monkey's gonna be you
Got to lift it
Lift it
Lift it off your back

Higher
You got to lift it
Higher
You got to lift it
Higher
You got to lift it
Lift it
Lift it off your mind

*(The instant the **GUITARIST** finishes [or a moment before] the **DRUMMER** takes over, his drum roll summoning the characters from the darkness. The **DRUMS** crescendo and end with a flourish. Silence.)*

HUNGRY TOWNSPERSON. It was September and there was a Town

ALL TOWNSPEOPLE. Erwin, Tennessee

BALLET GIRL. There was a Circus

RINGMASTER. Sparks World Famous Shows Proudly Presents –

STEAM SHOVEL OPERATOR. There was a Railroad

ENGINEER. The Clinchfield and Ohio

YOUNG TOWNSPERSON. There was an Elephant

ALL CIRCUS. Mary

ALL TOWNSPEOPLE. Mary

ALL. Mary

TOUR MANAGER. And there was a Man with Red Hair.

(A train whistle.)

ENGINEER. It was September and there was a Town and a Circus.

RINGMASTER. Charlie Sparks. Owner, operator. Sparks World Famous Shows.

You want to run a circus? Always keep it about the money. That's what Daddy taught me when I sat up till midnight counting pennies with him in the ticket car. Back when Sparks was his. Always keep it about the money.

Oh, you might have a dream – a dream of making a crowd leap to its feet, clamor with one voice, "Sparks, Sparks, Sparks!" – a dream of joining the pantheon: Ringling...Barnum...Bailey...Sparks.

But be careful. You're the Ringmaster. Dreams aren't for you. Dreams are for rubbernecks. Dreams are for suckers.

(The **HUNGRY TOWNSPERSON** *eats from a bag of peanuts, as he does throughout the play.)*

HUNGRY TOWNSPERSON. Erwin. The town that couldn't remember its own name. True story. S'posed to be named Er-*vin* after some rich fella. Postmaster messed up, spelled it E-r-w-i-n instead. Nobody remembered to fix it.

Yep.

That's Erwin for you.

STRONGMAN. I lift things.

Heavy things.

Anything.

This gets me on boat.

This gets me to America.

This gets me to circus.

STEAM SHOVEL OPERATOR. Never been nowhere.

Work a steam shovel down at Erwin railyard. Dig holes all day.

One...hole...after...another.

Papers say we might go to war with the Kaiser? I'll be the first to sign up.

"Oo-ee, what a patriotic young man."

Hell.

Ain't patriotic. Just bored.

(A drum roll building to cymbal crash as lights up on...)

BALLET GIRL. Ballet Girl.

(She strikes a fetching pose to a tinkling of cymbal.)

Ballet Girl.

(Another pose and cymbal.)

Ballet Girl.

(Another, to a cymbal crash, then rude drum thump.)

BALLET GIRL. *(cont.)* Can't dance. Practically old enough to have a girl of my own. But Ballet Girl it is.

Not a show girl, a Ballet Girl. Substitute "ballet" for "show" and I'm not a scandal; I'm an artist. I'm not a temptress in tights; I'm a dancer. We walk the wire, we Ballet Girls – between decency and lewdness. I need to find my balance.

The name is a start. And then…the smile.

(She smiles, a dazzling smile, the smile of a summer we thought we had forgotten. A shimmer of sound.)

Of an innocent flower.

(Shimmer.)

Spotless, pristine, blameless.

(Shimmer.)

Mm-hm. That's me. From head to toe.

MUDDY TOWNSPERSON. Mud.

Yella mud.

Everywhere.

Boardwalks help some. Not enough.

Always scrapin' it off yer shoes.

Enough to drive a person crazy, all that scrapin'.

Buried two kids in the mud…husband. Mud tryin' to swallow me up, swallow this whole town up. God's punishin' us for somethin'. Take another flood to wash Erwin clean.

PREACHER. I finished puttin' up the Erwin Evergreen Free Will Church in July. Turns out I mighta been a bit optimistic about how many rows of pews I needed. Little quiet on Sundays.

Love…forgiveness…joy.

I'll keep on testifyin', but…there's nothin' more lonely than a New Testament preacher in an Old Testament town.

TRAINER. It's love.

Feed her, wash her, sleep with her. Hell, end of the day, I even have a drink with her. Pour some whiskey in her bucket, mix it with some water – she loves it. Sticks her trunk in, it's gone in a second.

I'm lucky. They live a long time. You play your cards right, you got a friend for life.

YOUNG TOWNSPERSON. Could use more friends, I guess. Play with my brother Eli.

Skip stones at trains.

Read Tarzan books! He's somethin'. Read 'em right before bed. Gives me the best dreams.

(The **CLOWN** *enters, performs his routine to drum accompaniment. At its conclusion, he waits for applause, laughter. Nothing. He dismisses the audience.)*

CLOWN. Too old, the lot of ya. *(the Young Townsperson)* Kids laugh. Easy peasie.

And we joeys give kids more than laughs. Give 'em perspective, a lesson to carry forever, biggie: that there's always someone worse off than you.

(A "ba-dooom-ching" from the **DRUMS.** *)*

Except for us. Nothin' below a clown. They all pull rank, even the ballet girls. We're the last ones to get the make-up mirror – even though we use the most make-up.

("Ba-doom-ching.")

Let me put it this way: How many Ringmasters does it take to change a lightbulb? None. They tell the clowns to do it.

("Ba-doom-ching.")

MARSHAL. Erwin. Risin' taller every year. Best this country has to offer.

Peaceful. Keep it that way.

MARSHAL. *(cont.)* Folks 'round here honest, law abidin'.

Ain't the folks 'round here I worry 'bout. It's the strangers. It's that damn train station.

TOUR MANAGER. All the travelin' from town to town – all the firin', hirin': me.

Firin' happens all the time. Fella's lucky: he gets fired in one of the towns during a stop. Unlucky: he gets red-lighted: tossed off our train while it's movin'. Sucker don't see nothin' but the red lights of the caboose as it fades away.

And hirin'. Yeah. Do a lot o' that, too. Circus needs plenty of muscle – and not just in the ring. Townies get out of line now and then – want to prove they're tougher than the Strongman, get fresh with a ballet girl. Sparks sees any funny business, he calls out the "Hey Rube." I gotta teach every new hire: they hear that "Hey Rube," they drop whatever they're doin' and defend their own.

And that's just the tip – I gotta keep track of everything: people, animals, lumber.

Hell, we're like a little town of our own – carryin' all our buildings on our back.

(A train whistle sounds.)

MUDDY TOWNSPERSON. It was September and there was a Town and a Circus and a Railroad.

(The ENGINEER *listens to the whistle, examines his pocket watch, smiles in satisfaction, and puts the watch away.)*

ENGINEER. The Railroad invented Time in this country. Before us, there was chaos. Every clock for itself. People set clocks to the sun like cavemen, every town in America declaring its own Noon. We came along and told this country: no. We have a schedule to keep. Time is not relative; Time is precise. Time is not grey; it is black and white.

ENGINEER. *(cont.)* The Circus favored our proclamation. Before we came along, Circus traveled by wagon. Limped into town at any hour of the day, covered in mud and hog scat. The Railroad changed all that. They could depend on us. We're the metronome. We're the click-clack click-clack click-clack that lulls them off to sleep at night – men, horses, elephants – they all sleep with us in their ears. Click-clack click-clack click-clack. Like a second hand. On time. Always on time.

And Erwin? Without us, Time will pass them by. They need us just as much as the Circus. Not every town gets a train station. With a station, Erwin might become special, stand out, have a ribbon 'round its neck. Industry, progress – we can bring it all to their doorstep. Without us, Erwin'll be just another tiny town in Tennessee, a town nobody's heard of.

The Circus, Erwin, they have our guarantee:

You can depend on the Railroad.

(The train whistle sounds. The **ENGINEER** *checks his watch, smiles again.)*

HUNGRY TOWNSPERSON. It was September and there was a Town

RINGMASTER. There was a Circus

ENGINEER. There was a Railroad

TRAINER. And there was an Elephant.

(The **GUITAR** *plays a simple nostalgic tune, underscoring the Townspeople's description of the Sparks poster:)*

HUNGRY TOWNSPERSON. Mary

YOUNG TOWNSPERSON. We dreamed her before we saw her

MUDDY TOWNSPERSON. She was plastered on every telephone pole

STEAM SHOVEL OPERATOR. Every fence post

MARSHAL. Every barn door

PREACHER. September

YOUNG TOWNSPERSON. The Circus was coming

HUNGRY TOWNSPERSON. She was coming

MUDDY TOWNSPERSON. To our muddy town

MARSHAL. It was all there in black and white

STEAM SHOVEL OPERATOR. And color

PREACHER. It said:

(*Drum roll takes over as the* **GUITAR** *cuts out.*)

RINGMASTER. Ladies and Gentlemen, Children of All Ages, Sparks World Famous Shows
The Show that Never Broke a Promise

BALLET GIRL. Moral, entertaining, instructive

TOUR MANAGER. Twenty-five years of honest dealing with the public

STRONGMAN. Proudly presents a tremendous exhibition of wealth and splendor

CLOWN. All new for 1916

TRAINER. Starring Mary: the largest living land animal on Earth

STRONGMAN. Death defying feats of skill and daring

BALLET GIRL. Mary: over five tons

TOUR MANAGER. Two packs of man-killing lions

STRONGMAN. Mary: three inches taller than Jumbo

TOUR MANAGER. Five thousand seats

RINGMASTER. Mary: guaranteed at every performance

TRAINER. A free street parade each day at noon

CLOWN. Mary

TOUR MANAGER. Mary

STRONGMAN. Mary

BALLET GIRL. Mary

TRAINER. Mary

ALL. Mary
Mary
Mary
Mary
Mary
Mary

RINGMASTER. An elephant is an investment.

You open up your pocketbook, you throw down the eight grand, don't think about it again. Simple.

You've got the trained seals, the trapeze, the Strongman. Fine, but they aren't the bread and butter. No rubberneck comes to a circus doesn't have an elephant. Strike that. No rubberneck comes to a circus doesn't have a *big* elephant. Ever since Barnum and that damn Jumbo…

Jumbo was big, yes. He was big, the biggest. Not as big as the freight train that hit him, but big.

Now, Barnum understood investments. Sued the train company for insurance. Pocketed that, turned around and paraded the stuffed corpse across the country, charged money for *that*…until it started to fall apart, 'till he couldn't rightly call what he had left an elephant, 'till he was paradin' around a ten-ton ghost.

TRAINER. They love a parade. All elephants do in the wild anyway, walk around. Wild elephant herd follows the leader and the leader is the biggest female. I got no reason to mess with that here.

So, they all march behind Mary. Shadrack, Penny, Sue, little Mabel, one behind the other, trunk wrapped around the tail in front of her. All females. Easier. Males go into heat, go nuts. Not worth the trouble.

Easier to stick with the women, take a stroll with my gals. Let me tell ya, only thing better than watchin' an elephant parade is bein' in the elephant parade. Only thing better than bein' in the elephant parade is leadin' it. A dream. Sittin' on top of the world – little Shorty – on top of my own personal mountain, on top of Mary, legs wrapped around her back, head in the clouds.

(Drum roll. The **STRONGMAN***'s entire body trembles as he holds a heavily weighted barbell over his head. Cymbal crash.)*

STRONGMAN. Impressive, no? No?

So tell me.

I do not cost as much.

I am not as temperamental.

I do not shit all over the stage.

So tell me – please – have the courtesy to inform me:

Why is that elephant the star of the show?

(Drum roll, cymbal crash. The **BALLET GIRL** *strikes a pose as if she's in Mary's trunk.)*

BALLET GIRL. My name, my smile – they buy me some wiggle room. Wiggle room I need. Because once I'm decreed safe, nothing more than a wholesome Ballet Girl, then…I add the elephant.

Five tons of grey flesh bearing me half-naked into the ring, wrapped up tightly in its trunk.

That's right.

The innocent object of desire wrapped in a ding-a-ling ten feet long. And the best part? That trunk is always up. Bad luck to let a trunk droop in the circus, first thing an elephant learns.

Oh, I'm never more powerful, sensual, dangerous, than when I'm with Mary. Keep your spangles, your makeup, your headdress. Diamonds? Diamonds are nothing. An elephant is a girl's best friend.

TOUR MANAGER. They're not just for show. Hardest workers I got. Shorty acts like that's not parta their job description, but – once that train stops in a town – they're mine. Get 'em to load and unload the boxcars, push up the tent poles…those sons of bitches can do anything.

CLOWN. *(juggling)* Nobody looks down on the elephants. Right? They don't have to put on make-up or play the dope to get applause. They're too mighty to ever be made humble, too strong to ever be broken, too big to ever be laid low.

CLOWN. *(cont.)* And Mary's the biggest we joeys've ever seen. So we love her the most.

RINGMASTER. So when an opportunity comes along, you learn to not ask too many questions. Ringling tells you they got a tusker for eight thousand, you don't probe. Don't wonder why she's suddenly not worth so much. Could be anything. Maybe panicked one night, maybe ran outta the ring, maybe hurt somebody. Maybe, maybe, maybe.

Here's the thing.

Doesn't matter.

She's big enough, it doesn't matter what she did. You change her name – to say, Mary – and guess what? You got yourself a brand-new star.

Listen.

An elephant is not its actions. An elephant isn't cute, isn't a friend, isn't a symbol for something else. An elephant is an elephant.

And an elephant is an investment.

(Train whistle.)

CLOWN. *(counting on fingers)* It was September and there was a Town and there was a Circus and there was a Railroad and there was an Elephant and...ah! Last but not least...there was a Man with Red Hair.

BALLET GIRL. Kingsport. The menfolk loved us in Kingsport. I mean loooooooooved us. Joeys had to mop up all the drool afterwards. Mary and I triumphantly exited the tent after our act, to a chorus of catcalls.

TOUR MANAGER. Tennessee started off with a bang: we killed 'em in Kingsport. Circus can tell how it goes over by how many locals want to run away with it afterwards. Fifteen? That was a record.

Ten of 'em were six or seven years old, went back to mommy, but five were all right. Big, tough. Could be help with the next Hey Rube.

BALLET GIRL. I was giving Mary a celebratory smooch when this tall guy came out of the shadows and started walking towards me, mouth open, like he was hypnotized. Had these intense blue eyes and bright red hair.

I put on my innocent smile while I looked around for muscle in case the guy was trouble.

Nobody else in sight.

I kept smiling, ready to run.

And then I saw it.

He wasn't looking at me – he was looking at Mary.

(laughing) I let out my breath. He was 'bout 25 or so, but he looked like a kid while he stared at her. That glow – reminded me of when I started out.

I asked what I could do for him. He pointed at Mary. Said, "hey. I wanna join up. How do I join up?"

TOUR MANAGER. A ballet girl brought over this guy – hilarious. Shocka red hair, like a clown, one foot in the circus already.

Tell him I got lots of newbies to choose from here, lots of First of Mays. Why pick him? Tells me he's good with animals. I says, "okay, good with animals, good. How are you at shovelin' up their shit?"

Flinches, then he says, fine.

Steer him over to the horses. He says, no, I want to work with the elephants, I have to work with the elephants. I tell him, your funeral, Red. Elephant shit's the heaviest shit there is.

STRONGMAN. Lou walks by with this red-haired man.

Another First of May.

Another beanpole.

Why bother hiring these weaklings?

CLOWN. First of May walks by with Lou. Red hair, 'bout twenty-five, six.

Uh-oh. Trouble. Twenty-five? I tell him to stick out his tongue and say, "ah."

CLOWN. *(cont.)* "Ahhhhhhhhhh."

Aha! Diagnosis: circus fever! Terminal case.

(Ba-doom-ching.)

The guy blushes and Lou laughs and pulls him toward Shorty's car.

He's got the fever, all right. But a little late. A grown man followin' a kid's dream?

TRAINER. Lou knocks on my car, tells me I got a new roommate. Goofy-lookin' red-haired guy. I tell Lou, crowded enough in here with five elephants, but he insists. Tells me Red's my new partner.

Don't like partners. Partners don't have the patience. First of May who has it in his head he's gonna be a big tusker trainer? My gals deserve better. They deserve me.

But I'm not gonna be a jerk about it. I show Red his corner. He gripes about the smell and I tell him get used to it. Townies think elephants smell bad in the ring, try sleepin' with one in a boxcar. He shuts up when he sees Mary, looks at her like she's the answer to his prayers.

I don't know what's wrong with the guy – if he's a nut or soft in the head or what. Any case, I ain't gonna turn my back on him. I may not be big, but...if he makes one wrong move, Red's gettin' the red-light.

TOUR MANAGER. Shorty. Poor sap wanted to bite my head off. *(laughing)* So easy to rile up – like a mama hen.

Slammed the door and the train started up. We left Kingsport, for Erwin.

(The ENGINEER appears and smiles, looking at his pocket watch.)

On time.

(A train whistle.)

RINGMASTER. Once you start moving, Lou comes into your car, tells you your advance men wired back good news, said Erwin hasn't seen a circus in years.

That's what you want to hear. Whether it knows it or not, Erwin's been saving up, Erwin's been starving for cotton candy, popcorn, pink lemonade, whatever your candy butchers can shovel into their kissers. Towns like Erwin're gold, where your elephant becomes what she was born to: a five-ton cash register.

ENGINEER. Click-clack click-clack through the night. Their boxcars, our engine, our rails.

Erwin is waiting and we will not disappoint.

You can depend on the Railroad.

STEAM SHOVEL OPERATOR. Dig.

Dig.

Dig.

Dig.

Dig.

Lunch.

Dig.

Dig.

Dig.

Dig.

Dinner.

Home.

Drink.

Tired.

Drink.

Ache.

Drink.

Nothin'.

Drink.

Nothin'.

Nothin'.

Drink.

(The **GUITARIST** *and* **DRUMMER** *create the sound of the circus train approaching: hope, joy and a pinch of Johnny Cash.)*

STEAM SHOVEL OPERATOR. *(cont.)* Train.

Whistle.

Elephant.

(He smiles.)

Circus!

(The Circus folk transform the space in some fashion, creating a sense of the Big Top arriving.)

YOUNG TOWNSPERSON. Eli woke me up at 4:00 a.m.

I cussed him out – thought we was gonna be late.

Peeped in at our folks, still sleepin'. Snuck out the window, ran as fast as we could to the field where they'd do it.

We were all there, all the kids in Erwin, there to watch 'em set up the Big Top. The Greatest Free Show on Earth.

Train whistled, brakes screamed, men and animals stomped outta every door. Everybody marched around, seemed to know what they're doin' 'cept this red-haired guy…he kept bumpin' into stuff, trippin' on ropes. People yelled at him and his face turned as red as his hair. Funny. 'S'like a clown.

Then this elephant came out…I 'bout pissed myself. Bigger than the one we saw a few years back, lots bigger. Never saw nothin' this big. It made this big trumpet? We 'bout pissed ourselves.

The men unloaded the main tent pole and set it right between that thing's eyes. It walked on forward – boom, boom, boom – pushin' the pole up in the air as it stomped: higher, higher, higher. Holdin' that pole up there so the men could fix it in place.

YOUNG TOWNSPERSON. *(cont.)* Was like a dream.

Loud dream I guess, fulla hammerin' and poundin' and cursin'. Like watchin' an entire city get built in two hours.

That's 'bout my favorite parta the circus. Watchin' 'em set up. That and the parade.

Was really lookin' forward to that parade.

MARSHAL. 'Bout nine a.m. Ringmaster cleared the route with me. Told me to keep the horses away. Could spook the elephants.

Yes sir, yes sir, whatever you want, sir. Main Street will hold its horses.

Hell.

Not enough I gotta let the circus come to town and pick the pockets of all'a us. I got to roll out the red carpet for 'em while they do it.

HUNGRY TOWNSPERSON. Got myself a soda pop and a front row spot. Fella never knows how many parades he's got left in him. Have to make each one count.

MUDDY TOWNSPERSON. Glad I got there when I did – it was early, but street was fillin' up.

James.

Was there for James and the kids.

They always loved a circus parade.

TOUR MANAGER. It was his childhood dream.

TRAINER. I'd shown Red how to feed her, groom her, that's it. That's all he knew.

TOUR MANAGER. That Red came up to me right before the Erwin parade started. Asked me real polite-like.

TRAINER. One day? One day?

What the hell can you learn in one day? At anything?

TOUR MANAGER. Chance to get Shorty all worked up –

TRAINER. In India, guy stays with an elephant his whole life, like a goddamn marriage.

Here...Lou waltzed in – says,

TOUR MANAGER. Big deal Shorty, he wants to ride Mary in the march. Back off and give the new guy a chance.

TRAINER. I'm thinkin' no. No. He can ride little Mabel, fine. Shadrack, even. But Mary?

TOUR MANAGER. You're on Shadrack, Red's on Mary. Is that a problem?

TRAINER. I shoulda said something. I shoulda told him she was mine.

TOUR MANAGER. He didn't say nothin'.

TRAINER. I didn't say nothin'. Just stepped aside. Maybe made a face. That was my big protest, a face.

TOUR MANAGER. *(laughing)* The kisser on that guy.

TRAINER. It's trust. Trust you build up over years, not one day. Every peanut, every bath, every pat on the trunk. It's trust. Love.

But Red didn't have time for any of that. Red had a parade to lead.

RINGMASTER. Shorty's on Shadrack, but he still has to make the call – they won't start walkin' for anyone but him.

(The RINGMASTER gestures to the TRAINER to start the parade.)

TRAINER. TRUNKS UP!

(Circus music as the parade begins.)

PREACHER. I opened the doors and the steps to the church were thick with people. Faces I'd never seen before. I was fixin' to thank Jesus for answerin' my prayers.

People weren't tryin' to get in, though. Steps were just the best place to face *out*. To see the parade. Provided a little height.

All there. Whole town was linin' the street: white, colored, man, woman, child, all there. Glow in their eyes, waitin' to see a miracle.

Well. If I couldn't provide that glow on Sundays...at least there was something that could.

(The next sequence spoken slowly, in awe and joy, as the parade passes in front of the Townspeople.)

MUDDY TOWNSPERSON. Right down Main Street. Our Main Street.

STEAM SHOVEL OPERATOR. Had the day off from the shovel. Everybody had the day off. Circus Day.

YOUNG TOWNSPERSON. Eli and I 'bout pissed ourselves.

MUDDY TOWNSPERSON. Elephants, clowns, tigers…all muckin' down our Main Street. Through our yella mud.

STEAM SHOVEL OPERATOR. Made Erwin look like somethin' for once.

YOUNG TOWNSPERSON. Could hear the brass band and bass drum for miles.

MUDDY TOWNSPERSON. Mud on alla them circus folk. Hems of their dresses, tails of their coats.

STEAM SHOVEL OPERATOR. Colors you never dreamed of.

YOUNG TOWNSPERSON. So long. Stretched on forever.

MUDDY TOWNSPERSON. Elephant had Erwin mud all over it.

STEAM SHOVEL OPERATOR. Our yella town gone all purple and silver and red.

YOUNG TOWNSPERSON. That big elephant was leadin' the whole thing. That goofy guy – red hair? He was up on her back.

ALL TOWNSPEOPLE. Mary
Mary
Mary
Mary!

HUNGRY TOWNSPERSON. Hogs. Hogs musta been spooked somethin' terrible to act like that. Those piggies used to the Life of Reilly, just gruntin' up and down Main Street, eatin' whatever falls to the ground. Erwin garbage collectors.

But not that day.

HUNGRY TOWNSPERSON. *(cont.)* That day a band was playin', people rushin' out, circus plowin' through the middle of town...no way them hogs ain't scared. Erwin Garbage Department on strike until further notice. Clean up your own junk, people of Erwin. We on strike.

And thus, the hogs left the prize, left the Holy Grail of Garbage untouched in the mud: a juicy chunk of watermelon.

That's when the dominoes start to fallin':

Elephant sees melon.

Elephant walks toward melon.

Elephant rider turns red.

Elephant rider encourages elephant to abandon melon.

Elephant ignores elephant rider.

Elephant rider is most insistent, to the tune of elephant hook across elephant head.

Elephant keeps walkin' toward melon.

Elephant holds up parade.

Elephant rider turns red.

Elephant rider breaks elephant hook across elephant tusk.

Elephant thinks.

Elephant decides she's had enough of elephant rider.

Elephant picks elephant rider off elephant back with elephant trunk.

Elephant trunk throws elephant rider into soda pop stand.

Elephant rider groans in rubble.

Elephant rider thinks it's over.

Elephant rider is wrong.

Elephant walks over to elephant rider and puts elephant foot on elephant rider head.

Elephant rider screams.

Elephant foot steps...on...down.

HUNGRY TOWNSPERSON. *(cont.)* Elephant rider head explodes like a melon.

Elephant rider turns red.

Elephant walks away.

Elephant rider don't.

Elephant, free of elephant rider, strolls on over and helps herself to some melon.

Simple.

Parade stops, man dies, elephant turns killer. All for a melon. All for the want of a hog.

(Chaos and screams as we re-enter "real-time." A gun-shot. Several gunshots.)

MARSHAL. Nothin'. Thing didn't flinch.

Somebody screamed. Townsfolk ran off in a panic.

Couldn't do nothin' but stand there holdin' my empty pop gun.

And that thing kept eatin' the melon, rippin' apart its little snack while that poor man's crushed head sat next to it, all opened up and leakin'.

The Ringmaster ran up and told me we'll settle this later. I told him yes we will. Then a little guy led that thing back to the fairgrounds while some carnies carted the leakin' fella off in one of them animal cages. Clowns washed the street down with buckets of water. Vanished.

Quiet for a minute, like nothin' happened.

Hogs came back, then the people.

Most of 'em were cryin'.

A few were laughin'. At me.

PREACHER. Folks lined up again three deep on the street, waitin' for someone to tell 'em what to do. I propped the church doors open, but no one came in.

STEAM SHOVEL OPERATOR. There was a pool of blood and brains in front of the post office.

YOUNG TOWNSPERSON. I heard his head crack open again. In *my* head. Sharp crack, then softer ones, one after 'nother. CRACK crack crack crack CRACK crack crack crack –

MUDDY TOWNSPERSON. She stepped on his skull. Crushed it. Sent another body into the mud.

PREACHER. No one came in.

STEAM SHOVEL OPERATOR. Couldn't stop lookin' at that blood.

YOUNG TOWNSPERSON. CRACK crack crack crack

MUDDY TOWNSPERSON. Town's cursed.

PREACHER. No one.

STEAM SHOVEL OPERATOR. Heard that fella was from Kingsport.

YOUNG TOWNSPERSON. Eli thought he knew him.

MUDDY TOWNSPERSON. Coulda been any of us.

PREACHER. No one.

STEAM SHOVEL OPERATOR. Carl said she killed two men in Virginia

MUDDY TOWNSPERSON. Seven men

YOUNG TOWNSPERSON. Eighteen

ALL TOWNSPEOPLE. Right on Main Street

STEAM SHOVEL OPERATOR. It can't just do that. Can it? Go 'round killin' people?

ALL TOWNSPEOPLE. Our Main Street

YOUNG TOWNSPERSON. Tarzan woulda stopped her. Tarzan woulda jumped on her back and stabbed her through the eyes and gouged out her brain.

ALL TOWNSPEOPLE. Right on Main Street.

MUDDY TOWNSPERSON. Eye for an eye. Eye for an eye and maybe God'll stop punishin' us.

ALL TOWNSPEOPLE. Our Main Street

(The following lines are spoken simultaneously and loudly.)

HUNGRY TOWNSPERSON. All for the want of a hog. All for the want of a hog.

PREACHER. No one comes in. No one comes in.

MARSHAL. A few are laughin'. At me. A few are laughin'. At me.

YOUNG TOWNSPERSON. That's what Tarzan woulda done. That's what Tarzan woulda done.

MUDDY TOWNSPERSON. Eye for an eye. Eye for an eye and God'll stop punishin' us.

STEAM SHOVEL OPERATOR. It can't just do that. Can it? It can't just do that. Can it?

(The simultaneous speech moves into –)

ALL TOWNSPEOPLE. Right on Main Street
Our Main Street
Right on Main Street
Our Main Street
Right on Main Street
Our.....

*(The **MARSHAL** rises above the crowd.)*

MARSHAL. It coulda ended there, but that wouldn'ta been right, that wouldn'ta been justice. Maybe my pistol didn't mean squat to that thing, but goddamnit, we'd find something that would. It wasn't walking away from this.

Erwin don't look kindly upon murderers.

HUNGRY TOWNSPERSON. Crowd breaks up and follows the Marshal into the saloon. Me and the hogs stand in the doorway. Hear talk, lots of talk. Talk about public menace, talk about what you do with rabid dogs, talk about what's right and wrong. Hogs and me look at each other. They grunt and walk off. I do the same.

PREACHER. I stared at the steps. The empty steps. I walked into the church and let the doors swing shut behind me.

(singing)

PREACHER. *(cont.)*

> *Standing on the promises that cannot fail,*
> *When the howling storms of doubt and fear assail,*
> *By the living Word of Christ I shall prevail,*
> *Standing on the promises of God.*
>
> *Standing,*
> *Standing,*
> *Standing on the promises of God my Savior,*
> *Standing,*
> *Standing,*
> *I'm standing on the promises of God.*

TOUR MANAGER. Tried to get in touch with Red's family, friends. Didn't have none.

TRAINER. Like he didn't exist except for us, like he was born to do nothin' but cause us trouble.

BALLET GIRL. Poor kid.

STRONGMAN. He was weak.

> Did not understand.
>
> You are on top of her, but she is strong one.
>
> Not you.

CLOWN. Us joeys said a few words and buried 'im at the fairground.

RINGMASTER. You still have a show to do that night. Must go on.

> DOORS!

(The **TOWNSPEOPLE** *enter the Big Top. They are dimly lit, indistinguishable, threatening.)*

TOUR MANAGER. I told Charlie, maybe we should keep Mary out, maybe the people'd forget. But he told me what I already knew:

RINGMASTER. They won't forget. Aren't coming to see the circus. Coming to see the killer.

TOUR MANAGER. He was right. Woulda been a riot if we kept her away.

(Drum roll, spotlight on the **RINGMASTER***.)*

RINGMASTER. Ladies and Gentlemen, Children of All Ages, Sparks World Famous Shows Proudly Presents –

TOUR MANAGER. Normal night we play up the danger, talk up the toothless tiger. Not this time. Brought Mary out like she was the most innocent a' God's creatures.

I'm thinkin': Look at her. Look at her. She's just a big, dumb animal. Can we agree on that? All a' Erwin is here, under one big tent. This ain't no killer. Please?

(Drum roll ends in cymbal crash. A gasp.)

BALLET GIRL. The two of us arriving into the ring didn't usually get a gasp, but…circumstances had changed.

I tried to draw the crowd's attention away from Mary. I licked my lips, tossed my hair, threw myself out there like a two-cent whore.

Nothing. Their trousers stayed creased. I was playing to a tent full of eunuchs.

Forget about the lust then. Innocence would win the day.

"Look at me, all of you. Here I am, all wrapped up, cuddled up in the very trunk that did the deed, and am I scared, am I trembling?

I am smiling."

(She smiles, her glorious innocent smile, to a shimmer of sound.)

Smiling.

(The smile grows in intensity and the shimmer becomes almost violent.)

The brightest beams of white forgiveness I could 'till I thought the corners of my lips would crack open and gush blood over the sawdust.

But it didn't work. Those people weren't there to forgive. They stood up and pelted us with popcorn. And then they made this sound….

RINGMASTER. Listen to that.

> It comes true. Your dream comes true. In a tiny town in Tennessee. Crowd leaps to its feet and speaks with one voice, shakes the air, makes it tremble.

> It's not the "Sparks, Sparks, Sparks," you dreamed of, but, oh…they scream 'till their lungs ache, louder than any lion's roar. Young and old united in one glorious moment of certainty. Their scream, their chant, their heart's greatest wish:

> "Kill it. Kill it. Kill it."

> *(The **DRUMMER** and **GUITARIST** create a continuous threatening pulse throughout the rest of the Big Top section, a pulse that sometimes explodes into loud bursts of sound.)*

YOUNG TOWNSPERSON. Everyone around us was throwin' stuff at them. So Eli and me wadded our cotton candy up into baseballs and tossed 'em hard as we could. It got louder. The Marshal and people were wavin' guns around. Everybody shoutin'. All 'cept the colored section.

HUNGRY TOWNSPERSON. No need to say nothin'. Erwin don't give you no vote. Best to keep your mouth shut.

YOUNG TOWNSPERSON. Then the clown started talkin'. Never knew clowns could talk.

CLOWN. No, no, no! Red was one of us. Part of the circus. He knew the risks. This doesn't concern you. You townies got no claim here. Military has its own court – so does the circus. The Circus Court of Appeals!

> *("Ba-doom-ching.")*

YOUNG TOWNSPERSON. This little guy came out –

TRAINER. She was favoring her left tusk! They have nerves in there, big ones, run down half the tooth.

> But I saw him, you all saw him hittin' her tusk with the hook, whackin' the spit outta it, tryin' to get her to behave, to stay in line.

> What's she s'posed to do? She stopped him. That's all. She stopped him!

YOUNG TOWNSPERSON. The Marshal and the new Preacher stood up –

MARSHAL. These carnies can talk all they want. We know what we seen. And the People of Erwin demand –

PREACHER. No.

No, we don't.

I didn't cast no vote. No vote was counted.

Don't stand there all huffed-up with false pride and tell me that the People of Erwin demand this elephant die.

'Cause I don't.

Or add that in, if you want. Say "the People of Erwin *minus* the Preacher."

But it doesn't have the same power, does it? Addin' that minus. Doesn't have the right ring.

But you have to, to figure some way to leave me out of it. I'm a person, God knows. But I'm not, I'm not the People. I'm not the –

MARSHAL. We know what we seen.

And the People, the People of Erwin demand justice.

YOUNG TOWNSPERSON. Louder! Then the Strong-man grabbed a barbell and started shoutin' at the Ringmaster –

STRONGMAN. Sparks! Call the Hey Rube! Call it! Sparks!

YOUNG TOWNSPERSON. But the Ringmaster didn't do nothin'.

STRONGMAN. They want to know? Let loose the tigers, the lions! The rubbernecks want to know who is stronger? Their puny chests, their straw hats – I will crush them all! Sparks! Call the Hey Rube! Sparks! Call it! Sparks!

YOUNG TOWNSPERSON. Fin'ly the Ringmaster raised his hand –

(*The* **RINGMASTER** *raises his hand.*)

And everything got quiet.

(It does. The **RINGMASTER** *speaks privately to us.)*

RINGMASTER. Now, eight thousand dollars is a lot to lose.

A lot to lose in a hick town middle of nowhere.

But investments get tricky when the people want blood.

Because it's not just Erwin. Your advance men wire back from your upcoming stops: Johnson City, Rogersville, Indian Ridge: your circus isn't welcome until that elephant is taken care of.

So.

Is she still worth eight thousand?

Is she still worth anything?

You could sell her to another circus if no one's looking. Get part of your money back, anyway.

But people are looking. And elephants don't just disappear.

The people know what they've seen and they know what they want.

And you?

You know what your Daddy would do.

So you do it.

(spotlight on the **RINGMASTER***)*

Ladies and Gentlemen, Children of All Ages – the Circus Understands. The Circus Understands Your Wishes. This Mary Matter Will Be Settled to Your Liking Tomorrow. And...and We are Open to Suggestions.

ENGINEER. We had the answer. We always have the answer.

At first, they chose not to listen to the whisper of our rails.

The Marshal knew shooting it with a pistol hadn't worked, so they talked about getting a rifle or better yet, a cannon, Civil War cannon from the nearby museum.

ENGINEER. *(cont.)* Click-clack. Wrong track. We whispered louder.

They talked about electrocuting it, frying it like some of them had seen in the moving picture Thomas Edison made. But that was copycat stuff, that wasn't dreaming big enough.

We whispered louder. Would not be ignored.

And somebody finally heard us.

The railyard. There's a crane there can lift 100 tons. Says so on the side of it, right there in black and white. Nothing grey can stand up to that much black and white. Now, something like that could do something special, something never been done before. Why, something like that could hang her. Hang her like any other murderer. She may be big, but that Railroad crane's bigger. Crane'll get the job done. Crane'll do the trick. Crane's the Railroad, after all.

And you can always depend on the Railroad.

(The **TOWNSPEOPLE** *disperse, heading home for the night.)*

MARSHAL. Hangin' suits me fine, I guess.

Still think the cannon would be better.

MUDDY TOWNSPERSON. Eye for an eye. Erwin'll fin'ly be clean.

STEAM SHOVEL OPERATOR. I'd'a never believed it. Erwin. Erwin is the place to be tomorrow. Ain't nobody else – I mean nobody – nobody else in the world is hangin' an elephant tomorrow.

So that's somethin'.

That's somethin' *we* got.

You want to see it, you get off your fat ass and come here for a change.

(The **TOWNSPEOPLE** *are gone.)*

TRAINER. So now Lou and Sparks need my help. So now Red is forgotten, there's just me.

I ask them.

I wasn't good enough to handle her while she was alive, but I'm good enough to help you kill her?

They say, however you want to put it.

What am I gonna do?

Walk away, leave 'em to figure this out themselves?

No.

I stay.

I stay 'cause if I don't, they'll mess it up. It'll be even worse of a spectacle.

Lou and Sparks are happy this is my answer. Smile and open their mouths.

I stop 'em.

I tell 'em, don't think I've forgiven you. Don't think that. I will never forgive you.

Well.

This, they're not so happy about.

But I tell 'em, go ahead, what's your question?

They ask how to get her out to the railyard tomorrow, how to lead her through all those people without all Hell breakin' loose.

I think.

I tell 'em.

Tuskers aren't stupid, they know when somethin's up. You have to make her think it's a normal march. She can't go out there alone.

Mary has to lead the parade, like it's any other parade. Shadrack, Penny, Sue, little Mabel, all of 'em. Walkin' trunk-to-tail like always.

Then what?

TRAINER. *(cont.)* Then this.

Then chain Mary's foot to the track under the crane so she can't move. Then Lou, you lead the rest of the elephants away, fast, before they smell the panic on her. Then somebody runs up Mary's back and puts the hangin' chain 'round her neck. Someone she knows, someone she trusts.

They look at me like I'm crazy.

I tell them to relax.

I tell them I'll do it.

MUDDY TOWNSPERSON. Finished the cake about midnight.

Not a big one, best I could manage.

Had to fix somethin'.

Wasn't gonna be the only woman empty-handed.

PREACHER. I couldn't stop thinkin' of the glow. Like pickin' at a scab.

I prayed for hours.

I tried to sleep but I closed my eyes and all I could see was theirs.

Glowin'.

TOUR MANAGER. Stayed in my boxcar all night.

'Fraid to see what Shorty's face looked like.

TRAINER. I give her a peanut. A bath. A pat on the trunk.

Bring her bucket after bucket of whiskey water.

Might help some for tomorrow.

Dull it, maybe.

Hope it won't make it worse.

BALLET GIRL. Shorty won't let anyone near her, so I wait till he falls asleep at her feet. Then I step over him and crawl into her trunk, stroking it. Mary cradles me, swinging me back and forth until I drift off.

YOUNG TOWNSPERSON. Eli and me stay up all night, whisperin' under the covers. He asks me if I'd read to him and I do till he falls asleep. I go to pee and hear cryin' through Ma's door. Cryin'! On the night before the best day ever. Can't figure her sometimes.

MARSHAL. Stop by Walter's and make sure he's gettin' the band together for tomorrow. Whole thing won't seem right without some music.

HUNGRY TOWNSPERSON. Erwin was lively that night.

Bars crowded, streets full of trouble. What would norm'ly be trouble.

I walked up and down Main Street, past every mean drunk in town.

Funny feelin'.

Never felt safer.

STEAM SHOVEL OPERATOR. Stay up till I don't know when with Carl and them. Drinkin' till I have to be carried home. Then I just lie back in bed with a big grin on my face.

Can't sleep. Can't stop smilin'.

'Magine that.

Goin' to the railyard in the mornin' and couldn't be happier.

ENGINEER. The crane is oiled and tested.

A small but appreciative crowd gathers at its feet to watch it swing its arm

left and right

up and down.

I smile.

These who are here now. At midnight. They understand.

(*The* CLOWN *juggles.*)

CLOWN. She's too mighty.

Too strong.

Too big.

They'll see.

Joke's gonna be on them.

STRONGMAN. Sparks will call it.

Tomorrow.

The Hey Rube.

He will not let this happen.

I must rest.

I must be strong.

He will call it.

RINGMASTER. You don't sleep.

You think.

You wish you could charge admission tomorrow, but…
this isn't your show.

It's theirs.

*(The **GUITARIST** plays/sings **You Got To Lift It**. As the
song plays, the Townspeople transform the space for their
"show" – removing, covering or transforming the earlier
Circus additions. The Townspeople also add items of
clothing such as a parasol or a more formal hat to their
attire. The Circus folk do the opposite, exchanging their
flashy costumes for a more muted look. The **ENGINEER**
remains the same.)*

GUITARIST.

Got a monkey on your back
You gotta lift it
I'm'a tellin' you now, Jack
You gotta lift it
Lift it off or before it's through
Only monkey's gonna be you
Got to lift it
Lift it
Lift it off your back

Higher
You got to lift it
Higher
You got to lift it

Higher
You got to lift it
Lift it
Lift it off your mind

(The song underscores the following, sans vocals.)

MUDDY TOWNSPERSON. Mornin' fin'ly came. Cake turned out fine.

HUNGRY TOWNSPERSON. Couldn't help but feel it – there was a spark in the air.

MUDDY TOWNSPERSON. Put on brand new shoes. Wanted to look my best.

YOUNG TOWNSPERSON. Ma told us not to go. But Eli and me? We was goin'.

MUDDY TOWNSPERSON. Got to the railroad tracks, saw I wasn't the only one gussied up.

PREACHER. I went to bear witness. To see the glow.

MUDDY TOWNSPERSON. Men in the only suits they owned. Women in their Sunday best, prancin' 'round with parasols like it was Easter.

MARSHAL. Never been so proud.

MUDDY TOWNSPERSON. All'a Erwin. Seemed like all'a Tennessee.

HUNGRY TOWNSPERSON. Quite a sight.

MUDDY TOWNSPERSON. People risin' outta the mud, standin' top of boxcars, top of cranes, coal tipples.

STEAM SHOVEL OPERATOR. Was sittin' in the cab of my steam shovel. Best seat in the house.

MUDDY TOWNSPERSON. Picnic baskets, food, punch.

MARSHAL. We were doin' it up right.

MUDDY TOWNSPERSON. Everybody was sharin' with everybody else.

HUNGRY TOWNSPERSON. I kept to myself.

MUDDY TOWNSPERSON. Laughin', dancin'.

PREACHER. Glow was brighter than the sun.

MUDDY TOWNSPERSON. All the kids were play-actin' what was gonna happen.

YOUNG TOWNSPERSON. Eli and me were 'bout pissin' ourselves.

MUDDY TOWNSPERSON. Saw some men drinkin'.

STEAM SHOVEL OPERATOR. I saw Carl and them havin' a good ole time down there behind a caboose.

MUDDY TOWNSPERSON. I took the bottle outta their hands, smashed it on the tracks. They looked at me like I was crazy. But I knew it was wrong. Wrong to sully the act with liquor.

MARSHAL. It was gonna be somethin'.

MUDDY TOWNSPERSON. Act had to be pure, clean.

YOUNG TOWNSPERSON. I couldn't take it no more.

MUDDY TOWNSPERSON. My cake was long gone and you could feel it – we were ready.

MARSHAL. I told Walter to cut it.

(**GUITAR** *stops.*)

RINGMASTER. You wait for the signal from Johnny Tin Plate.

(*The* **MARSHAL** *draws his pistol and fires it into the air.*)

RINGMASTER. You tell Shorty to go 'head.

(*The* **RINGMASTER** *gestures to the* **TRAINER** *to start the parade.*)

TRAINER. TRUNKS UP!

(*Marching* **DRUMS.**)

STEAM SHOVEL OPERATOR. The killer was in front. Them elephants marched out holdin' each other's tails with their trunks – like a parade or a line of boxcars.

MARSHAL. Why they hell did they bring those other ones out?

STEAM SHOVEL OPERATOR. They walked all through the railyard up to the crane and this short guy chained the killer's foot to a train track.

TRAINER. *(under his breath)* Now, Lou, now!

TOUR MANAGER. I grabbed Shadrack.

YOUNG TOWNSPERSON. Then the other elephants started makin' this sound. Like they knew once they left, the big one was gonna get it.

TRAINER. *(under his breath)* Get them out!

YOUNG TOWNSPERSON. Real funny sound.

TRAINER. *(under his breath)* Now!

YOUNG TOWNSPERSON. Sounded kinda human.

PREACHER. Lord.

YOUNG TOWNSPERSON. Like 20, 30 people moanin' full out at the same time.

TOUR MANAGER. C'mon! C'mon!

YOUNG TOWNSPERSON. Eli and me plugged our ears.

TOUR MANAGER. Finally got Shadrack and the rest of 'em outta sight.

MARSHAL. Finally.

YOUNG TOWNSPERSON. We took our fingers out.

TRAINER. *(calming Mary down)* It's okay, it's okay, it's okay. Ready?

Showtime, sweetie.

STEAM SHOVEL OPERATOR. Short guy ran up her back.

MARSHAL. The women were hidin' their faces, or pretendin' to.

YOUNG TOWNSPERSON. We was 'fraid she was gonna pick him up with her trunk like she did that red-haired fella.

STEAM SHOVEL OPERATOR. But she didn't seem spooked at all. The short guy hooked the chain 'round her neck, patted her back and stood up.

(The **TOWNSPEOPLE** *applaud.)*

PREACHER. The little man ran off and she was alone.

MUDDY TOWNSPERSON. Mud in between the folds of her skin.

YOUNG TOWNSPERSON. She looked scary.

PREACHER. Helpless.

STEAM SHOVEL OPERATOR. Confused.

MUDDY TOWNSPERSON. Guilty.

MARSHAL. Like a killer.

HUNGRY TOWNSPERSON. Like a queen.

YOUNG TOWNSPERSON. The Marshal looked up at the Engineer and –

(The **MARSHAL** *fires his pistol into the air once more.)*

ENGINEER. Time.

The Railroad controls Time.

I made it stand still.

The masses waited below with held breath to see if it was possible, if the Railroad could actually kill their elephant dead for them.

I smiled. A reassuring smile. You can depend on the Railroad.

I placed my hand on the hanging lever.

I gripped the handle hard, tasting the silent seconds, rolling them around in my mouth, knowing that this part, the before part, would be the best part of all.

And then I threw the lever.

And Time started up again.

(All gasp.)

The crane groaned, gears grinding and –

MARSHAL. Damn! If that thing don't lift off the ground! An elephant, for Chrissake!

MUDDY TOWNSPERSON. It rose up steady till it was standin' on its hind legs, tiptoe. Toe nails scrapin' the railroad track. Tiptoe…like it was doin' a trick.

STEAM SHOVEL OPERATOR. Well, we started clappin' again, and I flashed a big smile down at Carl and them, 'cause they'd bet me there was no way in Hell that elephant was ever going to leave Mother Earth.

MARSHAL. But then we started wonderin' why that thing wasn't goin' any higher up.

YOUNG TOWNSPERSON. Gears sounded kinda stuck.

PREACHER. I got to thinkin' maybe she's too heavy, maybe a 100-ton crane can lift 100-ton steel but not a 5-ton animal. Maybe an elephant's soul is too heavy, maybe her soul is as heavy as the rest of her.

HUNGRY TOWNSPERSON. But that wasn't it.

ENGINEER. It wasn't the crane. Crane could lift her. Crane could lift her fine.

HUNGRY TOWNSPERSON. It was a people problem, not a crane problem. People don't always remember so good, even a big crowd of people, even thousands of people. People tend to not remember the little details when they got a elephant hangin' in front of them. And nobody did. Nobody remembered to unhook her. Nobody remembered she was still chained to the railroad track, her foot was still chained to the track.

STEAM SHOVEL OPERATOR. So they were kinda rippin' her in half a bit, pullin' her leg at this weird angle, her leg tryin' to hold her down to the ground while the rest of her was headed up.

MUDDY TOWNSPERSON. Her leg broke – a bone 'bout as big as my whole body – breakin', I could feel it in my spine, my spine buckled, ached in sympathy, rang like a tuning fork.

YOUNG TOWNSPERSON. Eli started cryin'.

STEAM SHOVEL OPERATOR. Shoulda left then, I s'pose.

YOUNG TOWNSPERSON. Eli ran off.

STEAM SHOVEL OPERATOR. But I stayed.

BALLET GIRL. Baby

STEAM SHOVEL OPERATOR. Stayed to see 'em unhook her foot, lift her up again –

BALLET GIRL. Baby

STEAM SHOVEL OPERATOR. – to see her trunk flailin' about, jerkin' around every which way, stabbin' the air like crazy, tryin' to grab hold of somethin'.

BALLET GIRL. Baby

PREACHER. Think she was nearly gone, then. Or woulda been, soon.

RINGMASTER. *(whispered)* No

PREACHER. That is…if the chain hadn't broke.

TOUR MANAGER & STRONGMAN. *(whispered)* No

PREACHER. But it broke.

BALLET GIRL & CLOWN. *(whispered)* No

PREACHER. The chain 'round her neck broke.

TRAINER. *(whispered)* No

ENGINEER. It wasn't the crane. Crane could lift her. Crane could lift her fine.

HUNGRY TOWNSPERSON. Mistake number two. It was a chain problem, not a crane problem. Chain 'round her neck couldn't handle all that weight. Weakest link, right?

YOUNG TOWNSPERSON. The chain popped and she came crashin' down onto the railroad track with this sound like an oak tree crackin' in half.

MUDDY TOWNSPERSON. She broke her…I think she broke her hip. Fight kinda went outta her. Couldn't seem to move, couldn't get off her side.

MARSHAL. It was loose.

PREACHER. Free.

YOUNG TOWNSPERSON. That little guy who climbed her before started screamin' like he was the one fell down and he yelled out to somebody and they handed him a thicker link chain and I couldn't believe it, but he ran up her back again.

PREACHER. Christ.

YOUNG TOWNSPERSON. His face was all red and twisted up, but – he just ran up there. Hooked her up again and ran off.

STEAM SHOVEL OPERATOR. Nobody clapped this time. Didn't seem…fact, some people started leavin', some of the women leadin' the kids off, anyway. Most stayed. I stayed. Stuck it out this far, I figured.
So

PREACHER. So

MARSHAL. So

MUDDY TOWNSPERSON. So

YOUNG TOWNSPERSON. So

HUNGRY TOWNSPERSON. So

MARSHAL. Crane lifted it off its feet again – higher…

YOUNG TOWNSPERSON. higher…

HUNGRY TOWNSPERSON. higher.

YOUNG TOWNSPERSON. She made some noises, some…air just kinda puffed outta her trunk and then that…that was it.

(Quiet.)

MUDDY TOWNSPERSON. I let my breath out.

I breathed in, lungs searchin' for that sanctified air. Waiting. Waiting to be made clean.

But the air…it tasted no different. It was flat and stale and rank.

They hung that bitch for nothin'.

I still got mud on my shoes.

(The **MUDDY TOWNSPERSON** *disappears.)*

BALLET GIRL. Made that crane keep swinging her for twenty minutes longer than they had to. Townies were waiting for her to let loose a bellow, rip herself free. Something that big couldn't die, could it? Something that full of life? So they kept her up there. But she was long gone, history. And I know the instant she passed.

Bad luck to point down with your trunk. They teach them that first thing. Never point down with your trunk.

That's what they taught her.

But she didn't care about that anymore.

Looks like I …

(She tries to smile her smile, but it and the shimmer fall apart.)

I might need some diamonds after all.

(The **BALLET GIRL** *disappears.)*

MARSHAL. Look. Look at that thing swing.

There are people in this here country that'll tell ya that we've become a small nation, a nation of little people with little dreams, staring at the ground 'stead o' the stars.

Well, look at what we done did here today and then tell me that this country is dyin'. Look at what happened here today in Erwin and then tell me there ain't no more dreamers. We hung a goddamn elephant today. An elephant. We made the impossible possible. So pack up your grip and go if you don't love this country, if you can't see the glory that surrounds you, if you want to stay in the mud. 'Cause this is America, goddamnit. And we can do anything we dream of. Anything at all.

(The **MARSHAL** *disappears.)*

STRONGMAN. It dangles her effortlessly

Taunting me
I could never lift her like that
I could never lift her

I tried once
Just to see
I couldn't do it
Not to any of them
Even little Mabel
Even the baby

But there she is
Swept off her feet
Our star
By that

It mocks me
It mocks me
It mocks me

(The **STRONGMAN** *disappears.)*

PREACHER. I'd forgot about the rest of 'em. Everybody forgot.

But once the crane set that poor beast down on the ground, her sisters came lumberin' back into the yard. Quiet. Reverential. Walked right through the thousands of people gathered 'round like we were invisible. Marched right up and stood over her. Opened their mouths and...their prayers didn't make a sound, but the air felt like it was...like it was movin', like it was tremblin'.

Them elephants bent down and...they caressed that Mary with their trunks, like they were soothin' her, calmin' her spirit. Payin' their last respects.

That man – that little man – he walked over to the biggest one of the mourners, petted her, whispered somethin' in one of those huge ears and led her out. Other elephants fell in behind, grabbin' the tail in front of 'em, walkin' off in a funeral recessional.

I fell in too, brought up the rear – best be gettin' home, gather my notes. Glow was gone. Had a feelin' it was gonna be crowded on Sunday.

(The **PREACHER** *disappears, humming "Standing on the Promises".)*

TRAINER. I'm red-lightin' myself.

I'll settle down somewhere, work at a zoo.

Don't really matter.

I'll get older and I'll die.

And that'll be it.

It's your show now, Shadrack.

My spark...is out.

(The **TRAINER** *disappears.)*

YOUNG TOWNSPERSON. Ma gave Eli and me a good switchin' that night.

Wasn't the worst part, though.

Worst part was the dreams.

(The YOUNG TOWNSPERSON *disappears.)*

TOUR MANAGER. Johnson City was in two days.

(The ENGINEER *and the* TOUR MANAGER *lock eyes for a moment. The* ENGINEER *snaps shut his pocket watch.)*

We'd be ready.

(The ENGINEER *and* TOUR MANAGER *disappear.)*

HUNGRY TOWNSPERSON. Elephants got those brains like traps, don't forget nothin'. All those peanuts they eat, maybe. People? People got short mem'ries. Let go of a mem'ry just as soon as you give it to 'em.

But not me. I eat peanuts. Stops it all from blurrin' together. All them colored boys led out to the yard must blur together somethin' fierce, 'cause nobody ever talks about how they hung colored boys in Erwin. They just talk about how they hung an elephant. Damndest thing. Damndest thing.

Peanut?

(The HUNGRY TOWNSPERSON *disappears, leaving his peanuts behind.)*

CLOWN. Why…

Why did the elephant cross the road?

What did the banana say to the elephant?

How can ya tell if an elephant is sleeping?

Why did the elephant quit the circus?

How do ya make an elephant disappear?

(He picks up a shovel and digs Mary's grave.)

STEAM SHOVEL OPERATOR. Hey.

(The CLOWN *digs.)*

STEAM SHOVEL OPERATOR. *(cont.)* Hey!

(The **CLOWN** *digs.)*

Thick mud. Hard to bury a squirrel, much less a...

(The **CLOWN** *digs.)*

I got a steam shovel. I could dig the hole.

(The **CLOWN** *digs.)*

You hear? I could dig the hole!

(The **CLOWN** *digs.)*

Hey.

(The **CLOWN** *digs.)*

Hey!

(The **CLOWN** *digs.)*

That's what we got machines for in the first place, right? To help people? Make the job easier?

(The **CLOWN** *digs.)*

What?

(The **CLOWN** *digs.)*

What?

(The **CLOWN** *digs.)*

I could dig the hole! I could dig the hole! LET ME DIG THE HOLE!

(The **CLOWN** *stops digging. He rises, defiant tears streaming down his face. The* **CLOWN** *stares at the* **STEAM SHOVEL OPERATOR.***)*

Please.

(They stare at each other across the stage.)

(A moment.)

(Lights slowly fade on the two men and up on the Ring-master.)

(Train whistle.)

*(The Town hums **Standing on the Promises** as the* RING-
MASTER *steps forward.)*

RINGMASTER. It was September and there was a Town and
there was a Circus and there was a Railroad and there
was a Man with Red Hair and there was an Elephant.

There was an Elephant
An Elephant

—

You pack up the tent
You load the boxcars

You wait

You wait
After midnight, after the townsfolk have gone home
after the prying eyes of Erwin are closed
safe
safe
safe and asleep in their beds
sleeping with the certainty that their boogie monster
is dead
good and dead
that they can get on with their stupid fucking lives in
their stupid fucking town in their stupid fucking…

(The humming ceases.)

You wake up the Clowns.

You wake up the Clowns and put the shovels back in
their hands.
You tell them to dig her up.

You tell them to dig her up and saw off her tusks.

You tell them to saw off her tusks and you tell them to
bring them to you.

You have to see what you can salvage, what you can get
for them, for the ivory, the tusks.

An elephant is an investment.

(Sound of the steam train struggling to life. Lights fade on the broken **RINGMASTER** *as the train sound builds, ending with a long and lonesome whistle.)*

End of Play

ABOUT THE PLAYWRIGHT

GEORGE BRANT's plays include *Any Other Name, Elephant's Graveyard, Ashes, NOK, The Lonesome Hoboes, One Hand Clapping, Terminal One, The Royal Historian of Oz, Lovely Letters, Three Men in a Boat, Borglum! The Mount Rushmore Musical, Tights on a Wire* and *Night of the Mime*. His work has been produced and developed by Trinity Repertory Company, the Kennedy Center, the Playwrights Foundation, Capitol Hill Arts Center, the Playwrights' Center, WordBRIDGE Playwright's Lab, ATHE, Premiere Stages, Trustus Theatre, Balagan Theatre, Open Fist Theatre Company, Theatre 4, Perishable Theatre, the Drama League, the Disney Channel, Circle Theatre, Factory Theatre, Street-Signs Theatre Company, Prop Thtr, Hyde Park Theatre, the Guerrilla Shakespeare Project and zeppo theater company. His script *Elephant's Graveyard* was awarded the David Mark Cohen National Playwriting Award from the Kennedy Center and the Keene Prize for Literature. He has received writing fellowships from the James A. Michener Center for Writers, the MacDowell Colony, and the Blue Mountain Center. George received his Masters in Writing from the University of Texas at Austin and is a member of the Dramatists Guild.

OTHER TITLES AVAILABLE FROM SAMUEL FRENCH

SONG OF EXTINCTION

E M Lewis

Drama / 5m, 1f

**2009 Harold and Mimi Steinberg/ATCA New Play Award
— American Theater Critics Association
2008 Ted Schmitt Award for the world premiere of an Outstanding New
Play – Los Angeles Drama Critics Circle
2008 Production of the Year — The LA Weekly Awards – Los Angeles, CA**

Max, a musically gifted high school student, is falling off the edge of the world — and his biology teacher is the only one who's noticed. A play about the science of life and loss, the relationships between fathers and sons, Cambodian fields, Bolivian rainforests and redemption. Max Forrestal is going to fail Biology if he doesn't complete a 20-page paper on extinction by 2pm on Tuesday — but his mother, Lily, is dying of cancer, and school is the last thing on his mind. His father, Ellery, a biologist obsessed with saving a rare Bolivian insect, is incapable of dealing with his wife's impending death, or his son's distress. Max's biology teacher, Khim Phan, tries to figure out why Max is failing the class. Helping Max, however, pushes Khim into a magical journey of his own — from the Cambodian fields of his youth into the undiscovered country beyond.

"Critic's Choice...artfully balances its theme of mortality between the intimate and the macroscopic...explores inner psychological states with remarkable eloquence and clarity..."
—*Phillip Brandeis, Los Angeles Times.*

"The interplay of the three [views on extinction] in Lewis' smart and honest script is one small push away from collective transcendence"
—*Amy Nicholson, LA Weekly*

SAMUELFRENCH.COM

CPSIA information can be obtained at www.ICGtesting.com
Printed in the USA
BVOW04s0843120615

404086BV00009B/88/P